VETERAN OF THREE WARS

CHALLENGES OF WWII, KOREAN WAR, VIETNAM WAR

10/27/19
To Shiela
Best Regards
Manny Knox

MANUEL(MANNY) JAMES KNOX

Manuel(Manny) James Knox
32 Pembrook Lane
Willingboro, New Jersey 08046

Registered at Library of Congress Control Number 2019901299

Veteran of Three Wars/ Manuel(Manny) James Knox. —1st ed.
ISBN 978-0-9980363-0-4

Supported by Uncovered Story Publishing (uncoveredstorypublishing.com)

CONTENTS

Acknowledgement and Dedication.......vii

Letter to My Wife.......ix

Introduction.......xiii

Chapter 1 Growing Up.......1

Chapter 2 Joining the Military.......7

Chapter 3 Basic Training.......11

Chapter 4 Military Assignments.......15

Chapter 5 World War II.......19

Chapter 6 Special Hat.......25

Chapter 7 Korean War.......29

Chapter 8 Medical Training and Other Medical Assignments.......35

Chapter 9 Vietnam War.......49

Chapter 10 Military Services Award.......61

Chapter 11 Retired from Military.......67

Chapter 12 Advocating for Veterans.......75

Document Gallery.......77

Note Gallery.......91

Acknowledgement and Dedication

No achievement in my life has been without the help of countless individuals, known and unknown, and this book is dedicated to each and everyone of you.

To my late wife Madge Bunny Knox, who made it possible for me the experience the joy that I continue to. You are in heaven now, but I thank you for you for your compassion, prayers, encouragement and unconditional love and for giving wings to fly.

To my children Johnny, Belinda, Daniel and Marilyn who have made me a very proud father.

To my grandchildren and great-grandchildren, you make me smile.

To my fellow veterans whom I served side-by-side or those I didn't meet, thank you for your service.

LETTER TO MY WIFE

U. S. NAVAL AIR STATION
PATUXENT RIVER, MARYLAND 20670

IN REPLY REFER TO:

Mr Manuel J. Knox
Medical Department
NAS, Patuxent River,
Maryland. 20670

Mrs Madge Helena Knox
3228 N. 15th Street
Philadelphia, Pa 19132

My Dear Mrs Knox,

This is to inform you that you are the most loved lady in the whole wide world. As your Husband I think it is my own privilege to tell you that "I can't stop loving you" and I really think you already know this but I get so much pleasure reminding my sweet baby and "WIFE" that I love you so. Very soon we will be together and I will not be leaving you for the week to be by yourself until the next weekend. I know you will love this and I know we bo h have been waiting for this for quite some time.

My Darling Wife I want you to know that you and our children are the most loved and needed persons in the world to me, plus being everything that a man could want in a Family. It was so nice talking to you a few hours ago and I sincerely hope that the glowing love and affectations that we have for each other will continually glow and grow to the highest heights that any love could ever attain.

I close this short note by telling you that I love you very dearly and our children also.

Your Loving "HUSBAND"

Manuel

Manuel and Madge Knox Celebrating Love

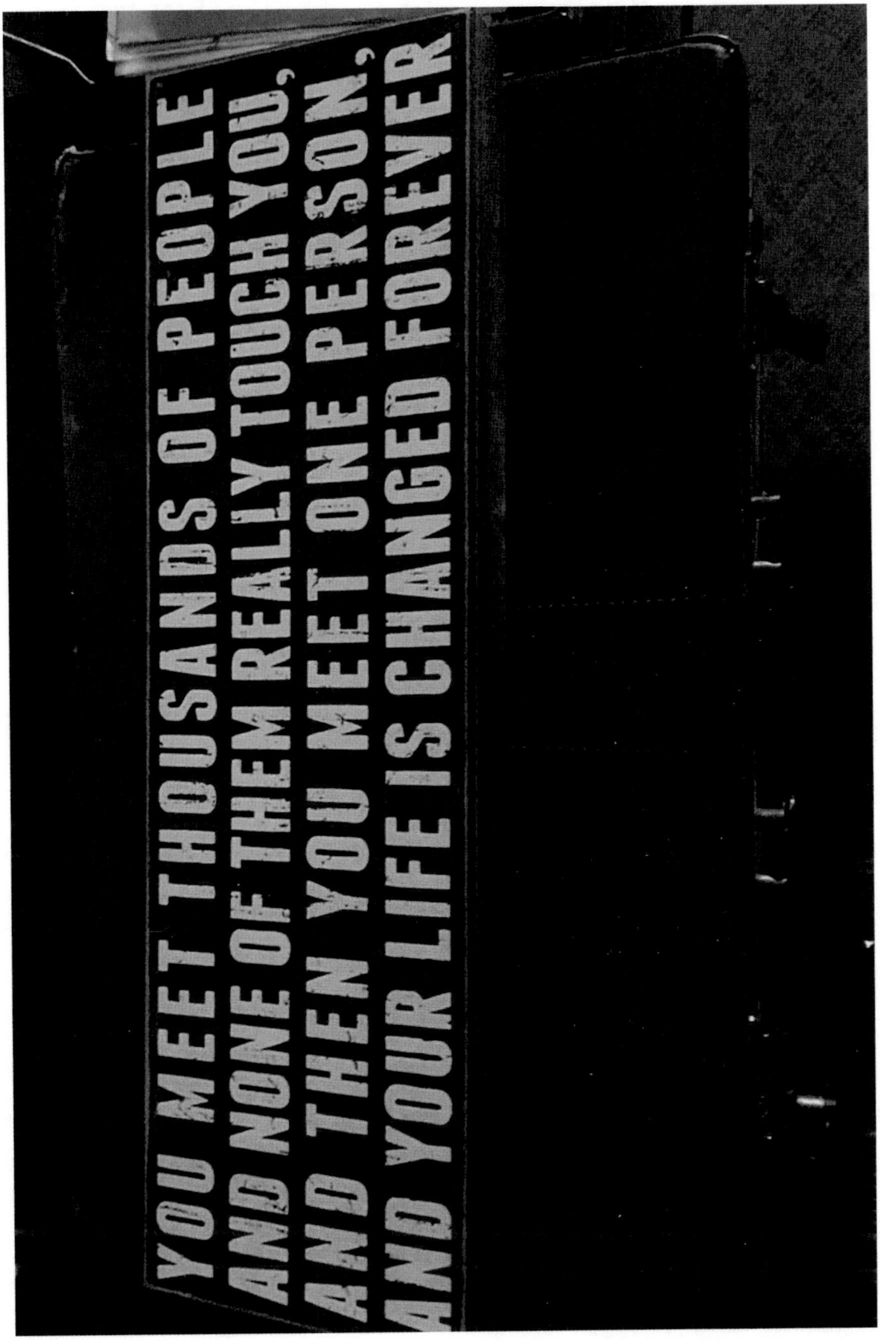
YOU MEET THOUSANDS OF PEOPLE
AND NONE OF THEM REALLY TOUCH YOU,
AND THEN YOU MEET ONE PERSON,
AND YOUR LIFE IS CHANGED FOREVER

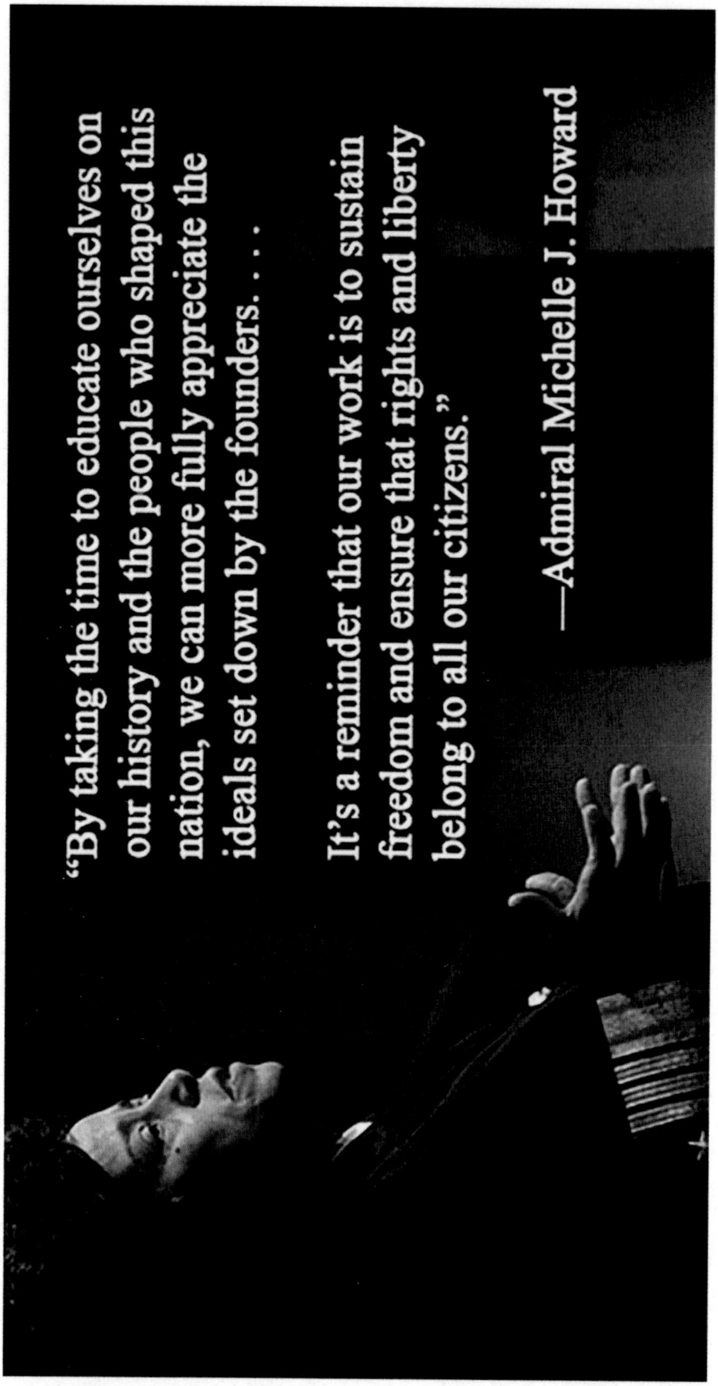
"By taking the time to educate ourselves on our history and the people who shaped this nation, we can more fully appreciate the ideals set down by the founders. . . .
It's a reminder that our work is to sustain freedom and ensure that rights and liberty belong to all our citizens."
—Admiral Michelle J. Howard

INTRODUCTION

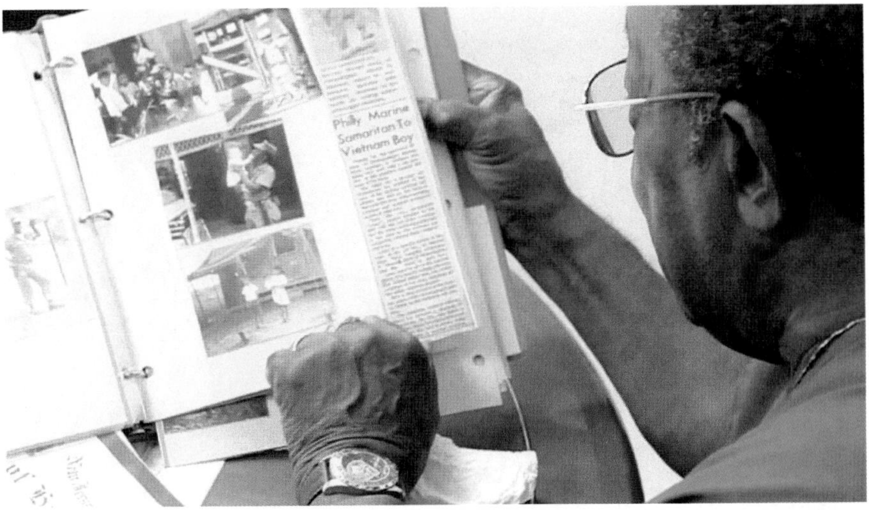

Anthony: Good afternoon, and hi everyone, and welcome to Uncovered Story. My name is Anthony Williams, publisher of Uncovered Story Publishing, and today I'm talking with a decorated veteran, Manuel "Manny" Knox, about the challenges of serving in three wars, World War II, Korean War, and Vietnam War. Welcome, Manny Knox.

Manuel: Welcome.

Anthony: Manny Knox is a well-known veteran who has graciously consented to share his story as an Uncovered Story. What a pleasure to have a conversation with a true American hero, fighting for freedom. Manny, thank you again for agreeing to this live conversation but most important, thank you for your service. Let's jump right in, so we can share your honorable service to America. I know a lot of family, friends and veterans want to know your story.

Ruby Tuesday Diner (Willingboro, NJ) server shows her appreciation to three war veteran, Manuel J. Knox by treating him to lunch for his service.

CHAPTER 1
GROWING UP

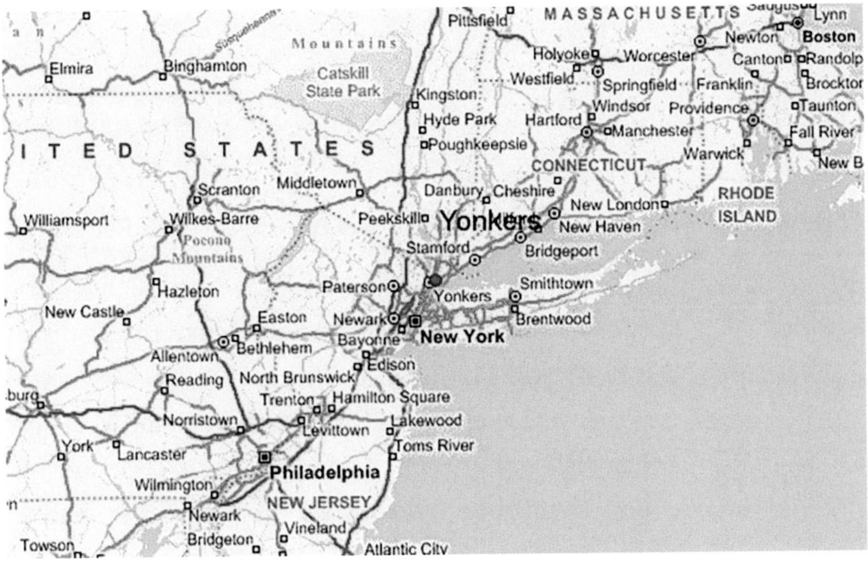

Manuel J. Knox hometown, Yonkers, NY

Anthony: I have a few general questions first about your background and experience, so first let's talk about chapter one, growing up. Where and when were you born?

Manuel: I was born April the 29th, 1925, in Yonkers, New York.

Anthony: Great, who were your parents?

Manuel: Edith and Elmer Knox.

Anthony: All right, great. What kind of jobs or occupations did your parents have when you were growing up?

Manuel: My father didn't have hardly anything, but my mother worked in a laundry, and she would prepare clothes which was delivered by bags to the laundry. They put them in the big machines, and when they come out, some of them had to be pressed and others had to be just fluff dried.

Anthony: Oh, okay.

Manuel: She worked quite a long time over there, and it was rough on her.

Anthony: Right, so she primarily was the single breadwinner in the family.

Manuel: Actually, my father died and I didn't even follow up on the history of him from the time that he died, and I don't even have a date, but she was painful. Things got a little tough with her, and we had to be, my youngest brother and my next oldest brother, had to be put in an orphanage in Riverside, New York, which was a short jaunt from Yonkers. We must have stayed there two or three years, and a family in Peekskill, New York, Mr. and Mrs. Rabb, kept coming by and they finally took us home with them to Grand Avenue, in Peekskill, New York. We must have stayed there about three or four years, then mom got on her feet in Yonkers and we came back to Yonkers, under where she had an address, 45 School Street, Yonkers, New York.

Anthony: Wow, wonderful.

Manuel: I outsmarted my older and younger brother, when the principal of Public-School Number Two asked the oldest, Clarence, "Where was you in Peekskill?" He was in the sixth, I was in the fifth, Elmer was in the third. Clarence said sixth, so they said, "Well, we'll try you in the fifth." She asked Elmer next, and he said, "I was in the third." They said, "Well, we'll try you first in the second." Listening to that, I got a wise bug in my ear. She asked me what grade was I in. I actually was in the fifth grade, and I said to her, "Sixth grade." She said, "Well, we'll try you in the fifth," and that was the same grade I came from Yonkers.

Anthony: Right.

Manuel: However, I did excel more in lessons. My both brothers, their character wasn't for school. One day, there was smell of meatloaf, something cooked in the classroom, because I wound up being in the same classroom as Clarence.

Anthony: Oh, right.

Manuel: The teacher walked around the room, and next thing you know, she started to she saw this shirt with all this oil on it, and he had taken a slice of meatloaf, and he didn't wrap it too good, and it fell into his shirt. That was the funniest thing at school. She had to send him home, but he made sure he ate his meatloaf.

Anthony: Right, so what were the names of your brothers and sisters?

Manuel: Clarence was the oldest, then Elmer was the youngest. Actually, my name was in the middle, so Elmer, Manuel and Clarence.

Anthony: Oh, great. Do you have any sisters?

Manuel: No, no sisters; foster sisters, yes, that Mrs. Rabb had. We tried to get in touch with her. Leila, she was the foster sister. She was very, very pleasant and smart. I guess we got to age about 12, 13, mom proved to them that she could take care of us, so we went back to ... We went from Peekskill, New York, back to Yonkers.

Anthony: Outstanding. Did any of your brothers serve in the military?

Manuel: Yes, Clarence served in the Army, and my mom had to call the shore patrol, the military police to come get him, because he was over the hill and she didn't know it.

Anthony: Oh, right.

Manuel: I got a weekend off from Willow Grove Naval Air Station, and I came home and Clarence was home. I go back, and I'm home, I'm away for another month, and I got a two-day pass. I come to see my mom. Clarence was still home. I said, "Mom, he ain't supposed to be home." She called, "You're right," and God willing, he could have been court martialed, because he had missed a ship to England. But, the officers in charge took care of him. They told him, "Never let it happen again," but he wound up getting a discharge in '46 when I got discharged.

Anthony: Okay, so what did you do before you entered the military?

Manuel: Believe it or not, I had a job at a fashion shop. I hated that. Mr. Kessler would have me help him dress the windows, and the mannequins were naked. Whenever we would do it, it just so happened boys from the school would be coming by, and I'd be dressing these mannequins. Of course, I wound up having a better salary than most of them, because salary was real low, but mine was a little more because I was doing an important job, and I delivered fur coats.

Anthony: Oh, okay.

Manuel: Silver fox jackets and all them stuff, and never had any problem with it. Then one day this lady, I delivered a silver fox jacket to this lady's house, and there was a space between her gate and her front door. She said, "Bring it up here." I said, "No," because a bulldog was in there. She said, "Bring it up." I said, "No." She said, "He won't bite." I said, "Has he got teeth?" I said I ain’t coming. So, she came and got the coat. In fact, that was my best tip of the day. I told her, "Lady, you ain't getting me to walk up there."

Anthony: So, you were working at the store while you were going to high school.

CHAPTER 2
JOINING THE MILITARY

Manuel: Yes, then I decided that I could do better in the military. At the time, there was draft cards, and my number was called up pretty fast, so I ahead of them, I went down and volunteered.

Anthony: Right, so that means, so joining the military, you were drafted.

Manuel: Yes, mm-hmm (affirmative).

Anthony: Okay, do you remember the day you enlisted or started?

Manuel: Funny thing, I do. I do remember. Now, let me see if I remember right looking at this.

Anthony: July 1943?

Manuel: Yeah, 15th of July, '43.

Anthony: July 15th, 1943.

Manuel: That's right.

Anthony: Wow.

Manuel: And since I already had military service, I didn't have to go to the boot camp.

Anthony: But you went to basic training, right?

Manuel: Oh no, you're right. Yeah, I did basic training.

Anthony: Right, so you went to basic training. I think you said you went to basic training the next day after you got drafted?

Manuel: Yes, I did. No, the next day after I-

Anthony: Signed up.

Manuel: Yeah, I went down to volunteer and signed up, yeah.

Anthony: So, any of your classmates sign up with you during it?

Manuel: He was supposed to, but he fooled me. He didn't go down. When I came back after that first 30 days in Great Lakes, Illinois, you got a pass to come home, I came home and saw him and he said, "Man, I thought you was kidding. I didn't believe you, you'll go down there." It was too late.

Anthony: Wow.

Manuel: Then he did go and join the Marines.

Anthony: That's amazing, so July 15th, 1943, you were drafted and the next day you were off to basic training.

Manuel: Oh, I had a draft card, so rather than let them call me and put me where they want, they gave you the prerogative of volunteering for the branch of service, so I said, "I want to go to Navy."

Anthony: Oh wow, okay, so that's how you selected the Navy.

Manuel: Yes.

Anthony: Right, so then you were drafted. You went and enlisted on your own, even though you had a draft number, and you joined the Navy.

Manuel: Yes.

Anthony: And then you went to basic training, and you went to basic training shortly after you signed up.

Manuel: Right, right.

CHAPTER 3
BASIC TRAINING

Naval Station, Great Lakes, Illionis- Basic Training, Manuel J. Knox was housed in Camp Lawrence of the three camps designated for African-American sailors

Anthony: So, basic training; let's talk about basic training, which is a section here. Where were you assigned for basic training?

Manuel: Great Lakes, Illinois.

Anthony: Great, Lakes, Illinois.

Manuel: They had three black camps there, Camp Lawrence, Camp Roberts and Camp Smalls. I was assigned to Camp Lawrence, and it was on the other side of the main building where the boot camp station was in Illinois, and these three camps were outside, like a highway. We were on one side of a highway, and the other side of the highway was Great Lakes U.S. Naval Training Station, Great Lakes. We would have to march from our thing over to the side, but whenever we went over to the side, the boys had to march with a rhythm. We would come across, and the white boys would be doing their work at their camps. When we'd get across that, they'd stop everything, watch us go through, because we had songs like (singing).

Anthony: Oh yeah, right.

Manuel: They would stop everything, and wouldn't do no work. They couldn't get no work out of them until we passed through.

Anthony: Outstanding, yeah, so-

Manuel: We'd go over and draw supplies, get fitted out for your shoes your jacket, shirt and all that stuff. Following at Great Lakes, we had, always in charge were white, but all the companies were black, and then some of the guys in the company who had college education, they got their rank higher and they were in charge. I got to be in charge of the marching group, because I liked to march. We would really do our number.

Manuel: We learned a special one that I brought back, after I was discharged I brought back to the American Legion Post 1017, and my youngest brother wound up being a commander, because he got out after me. However, at Great Lakes, a funny thing happened. I was standing in this line, and I was looking at the heads of the guys in front of me. I said, "Nobody could have a head like that. Elmer?" And he turned around, it was my youngest brother.

Anthony: Really?

Manuel: Two weeks after I went in, he went down and-

Anthony: And joined?

Manuel: Right, and volunteered to go, and they put him, he was in the company next to mine and I didn't even know it. Ironically, the same day that I met him, I got cited for a dirty hat and a dirty shirt, a mark on my shirt. We had inspection, and what happened is one of the fellows, guys could stick him in the side, and he was like what you call goosing. They would stick them in the side and walk away, and whoever was standing near him really got it. If you saw him, you would get out of the way, but I didn't see him. That guy turned and knocked me down.

Manuel: Can you imagine, in white? And we had white uniform, white hat, white shirt, white pants, everything. I tried to get in the barracks to change and the guy said, "You can't come in here now. Inspection is going on," so I dusted off as best I could and got back in the line. Here comes the inspection officer. "Knox, how come your hat and shirt are so dirty?" And I went and told him and he said, "No, you didn't clean." "Yes, I did, sir. I had an accident." I didn't tell him that the guy hit me. I said, "I accidentally got brushed away, and I fell and my hat went off."

Manuel: He said, "No, we're putting you on extra duty tonight," so like 4:30, five o'clock, all the guys take a shower and are going to get in the movie line or go to the canteen, I had to go meet the first class who was running us through calisthenics for doing bad. Elmer refused to do something in his group, and I looked over and he was in the other group, right next to it. Pretty soon the chief says, "Knox, you can go," and I started to go. He said, "Not you," because he heard him say, "Knox, you can go." I left, two hours later coming back from the movie, my brother was out there still because he wouldn't do it. He wouldn't do it right. Boy, they really got him.

Anthony: Wow, that's pretty amazing, so you were in basic training with your brother.

Manuel: Basic, yeah.

Anthony: And, what a surprise to you.

Manuel: What a surprise.

Manuel: One other thing, the chief petty officer was a white guy, and the commanding officer was a white guy, but we never saw black officers

Manuel: However, the first 13 black officers picked for the navy, one of them was from my company named Cathcard and he was a knowledgeable guy, and I think he was in his second or third year of college when they drafted him.

Anthony: So, this other thing I think people would like to hear about, let's just kind of recap some of your military history up to World War II. So, you entered the military July 15th, 1943.

Chapter 4
Military Assignments

Anthony You went to basic training shortly after that, and then let's talk about your next assignment. Your next assignment was that you were ... Where was your next assignment?

Manuel: Willow Grove.

Anthony: Willow Grove Naval Air Station in Horsham, outside of Philadelphia, Pennsylvania.

Manuel: That's right.

Anthony: Wow, okay.

Manuel: And a fellow from the Philadelphia naval station was the ferry command for planes going to Europe, and so they formed a guard unit, and you had four-hour shifts. Each person was responsible for 250 to 300 yards along the fence completely around that air field. Anybody came up to the fence and you challenged them and they didn't do anything, you called in but you fired a shot at them.

Anthony: Right, so you were a flight line guard.

Manuel: Yes, and each day you had to go in whatever time your shift was, 15 minutes before your shift you'd go in, and you go to the armory and draw your .45 out. You would show him that it was not loaded, click it off, and then load it and take it with you. When you came back, you had to take the clip out and point it up in the air and squeeze the trigger. We did that, and received a lot of commendations about some of the guys catching people trying to come over the fence. The next thing you know, I got orders to go to Hawaii.

MILITARY ASSIGNMENTS

Branch	**US Navy**	
Service Member	**Manuel(Manny) James Knox**	

Date	Assignment	Location	Duties	Rank
July 15, 1943	Draft	New York, NY		
July 16, 1943	Basic Training	Great Lakes, Illinois		
October 1943	Willow Grove Naval Air Station	Horsham Township, PA	Flightline Guard	Seaman 1st Class
1944 World War II	Naval Ammunition Depot	Hawaii	Ammuniti on Loader and Truck Driver	Seaman 2nd Class
January 16, 1946	Discharged from US Navy			
September 6, 1950 Korean War	Reenlisted in US Navy Assigned to USS Brinkley Bass DD 887	Wonsan Harbor, North Korea	Hospital Corpsman	HM3
September 1952	St Albans Naval Hospital	Jamaica, New York	X-Ray Technicia n School	HM2
1953	Naval Dispensary	San Juan, Puerto Rico	X-Ray Technicia n	HM2

Date	Assignment	Location	Duties	Rank
1956	Military Sea Transportation Service (MSTS)	Brooklyn Army Terminal, Brooklyn, NY	X-Ray Technician	HM2
July 30, 1960	Discharged from US Navy			
July 1, 1960	Reenlisted in US Navy			
1961	Armed Services Recruitment Station	Philadelphia, PA	Chief of Recruitment	
December 2,1964	The Bureau of Medicine and Surgery – US Navy	US Naval Hospital Portsmouth, VA	Advanced Hospital Corps School	HM2
June 15,1965	Field Medical Services School	Marine Corps Base Camp Pendleton, California	Combat Training	
September 23, 1965 Vietnam War	3rd Marine Division, Company B	Vietnam	Hospital Corpsman	HM1
December 7, 1966	US Navy Patrol Squadron VP-44	Naval Air Station Patuxent River, Maryland		HM1
January 5, 1968	RETIRED FROM US NAVY			HM1

CHAPTER 5
WORLD WAR II

African-American sailors loading ammunition at the Naval Ammunition Depot, Hawaii. Manuel J. Knox was stationed at this facility as an ammunition loader during WW II

Anthony: Well, so you went to, oh, Hawaii.

Manuel: FPO, yeah.

Anthony: Yeah, so you went to Hawaii, and that was in 1944. Let's see, naval ammunition depot.

Manuel: NAD (Naval Ammunition Depot)

Anthony: Wow.

Manuel: FPO 66.

Anthony: So, what was your job there?

Manuel: I'm in ammunitions.

Anthony: So, you were an ammunition loader.

Manuel: Yeah.

Anthony: Do you load them onto the ships?

Manuel: No, load them onto the trucks.

Anthony: Onto the trucks.

Manuel: The trucks, yeah. A tractor trailer comes in front of each mine, and they had groups. I'd be in group one, and they maybe had 10 groups. Each group had about 10 guys in it, and you would go down and load your trailer. After you load your trailer, that guy took off, another trailer would come up but you'd have a space of time to go have something to eat, come back, and then you'd come back and load them up. And then that guy that drove them trailers down to Honolulu, where the ships and the subs come in.

Manuel: The sub had a long, flat pier to drive out with. Most guys didn't drive out, because you couldn't turn around and come back out. You'd have to back out, so it was really nice to learn to drive a tractor trailer. It was up there in the hills Lualualei, and that was also an ammo dep. Navy officers come up and, "We need some tractor trailer drivers." Now, I drove the six by, but I never drove the tractor trailer, and I raised my hand up that I could drive one, because I wanted to get out of this group.

Anthony: Excuse me for interrupting, but you were loading all this ammunition by hand.

Manuel: Oh, yeah.

Anthony: And this was what, 40 millimeters?

Manuel: Well, it depended on what magazine you were sent. The main magazine I was sent to was projectiles for the battleships. The projectiles for the battleships was taller than each one of us, heavy, and what we did, we had a ...

Anthony: Hand truck?

Manuel: Hand truck, yeah. We had a hand truck, you would get your hand truck under it, and another guy would tip it back, and they'd bring a strap around it, then you'd wheel it out, so when you wheel it onto the flatbed, then there were other sailors that had two by four pieces of wood. They'll put them down alongside of it and drive the nails in to keep it from moving on the ship, on the tractor. And then when your tractor trailer got loaded, or did I say I got selected for the tractor trailer group?

Anthony: No, you didn't. So, when you raised your hand to be a driver?

Manuel: Yeah, they said, "Okay, come on," so I went down, and so there was one seaman named Baxter. He was good. He said, "I tell you what I'll do. I'll go out in the evening with you and give you clues on driving this tractor trailer." I went out with him, and he showed me enough that I passed the test. The person in charge of them had three tractor trailers together, just like putting three fingers together. He said, "Take the middle one out," and I took the middle one out and drive around, turned my corners good, stopped good. When we come back he said, "Put it back between the two of them trailers." I drove around in back and drove straight up between them. He said, "No, pull all the way out, and I want you to back it up between them." Now, that was the hardest part of the exam. I didn't think I had passed, but they finally passed me enough. I was better than some of the other guys taking the exam.

Anthony: Right, so this was during World War II.

Manuel: Yes.

Anthony: And in Hawaii.

Manuel: We went down, whatever night, weekend that you had or couple of days you had off, we would go down to a little town called Waikele Gulch. There I met a family that invited me every time I came out on liberty, to stop by and have dinner with them. Pretty soon, everything was going ... We got a lot of compliments and awards for really getting the ammo out. One morning, daylight, everybody said, "The war is over," and the biggest thing you could do then was count your points. You got a certain amount of points for every month that you were over there, and it didn't take long before I had the amount of points and told my mother, "I'm coming home." However, coming back from there-

Anthony: So, I have a question before you go into about coming back from there. So, you guys, you and the other black seamen, had to ... You still were segregated.

Manuel: Yes.

Anthony: And so, you were limited in some of the activities that you could do, both on the base and off the base.

Manuel: That's right. Now, I did leave out that when I got to the ammunition depot in Lualualei, the Army was doing so bad in the South Pacific that they took like half of your company and would train us to be logistics support men, and give you a carbine. They were shooting at each other at night, cops shooting at each other at night. They had to have MPs that was, the MP was Army, SP was Navy shore patrol, and they had to have shore patrol men running around trying to catch guys who were messing around with them carbines when they weren't supposed to.

Manuel: So, I got enough points and get in a ship to come home. Now, I made a lot of money, and I remember they had, we got to Frisco, I was really excited to just get me home. So, they take us on a ship from Frisco, and go all the way down to the Panama Canal and come up to New York, to Lido Beach.

CHAPTER 6
SPECIAL HAT

Anthony: Wow, so let me ask you something. So, I see this hat. This is your special hat.

Manuel: Yeah.

Anthony: So, that hat is World War II, Korea, Vietnam.

Manuel: Yes.

Anthony: Wow, what a tribute. So, when you were in during World War II, do you have any special friends or guys that you think about occasionally?

Manuel: Oh, yes. There was one guy, he would always, I'm trying to think of, I can't think of his name, but he would always walk up to you and say, "You got a cigarette?" and guys would give him a cigarette. The guys said, "Well, how come you don't buy your cigarettes?" And he would say to them, "Why should I buy cigarettes if you're buying them?" And yet still, when he'd come up and ask them for a cigarette, we would give him a cigarette. Of course, cigarettes were about five to 10 cents a pack. You can imagine what they are today.

Anthony: Right, so where was this when you ... I don't know where I heard this, somewhere, but when somebody made a bet with you?

Manuel: Oh, when we had the mess duty. Well, two things in mess duty; number one, you had to be the mess man for the chief's quarters in the morning, where the chief ate their food, but you had to do two weeks. So, I did my two weeks, and I didn't get relieved, so I asked one of the chiefs, "How come you didn't relieve me?" He said, "You make coffee too good." I said, "What do you mean, I make coffee too good?" He says, "When they find a guy that can really make the coffee, so that they have good coffee, he's going to stay." The next day all you can hear is Chief, "What's wrong with this coffee?"

Anthony: Wow.

Manuel: But they had taught me to put eggshells up to measure them and everything, and let the hot water run on them, and it made a difference to the coffee. I didn't know.

Anthony: Wow, that's-

Manuel: There was one guy there, I told him that the machine that runs the trays through, I said, "A human could go through there." He said, "I'll bet you can't." I said, "I'll bet you can," so they put the racks up there, and I like a little dummy got up there and laid across two racks and he started the machine up, and the catch got to going through. Halfway through, he turned the water on, and that water goes to 160 degrees.

Anthony: Oh, wow.

Manuel: When I came out the other end, I thought when I peeled my dungarees away that my skin was going to come away. I got outside of it, and pretty soon it's cool enough and everything. I said, "All right, give me my $20." He said, "I didn't have no bet with you." Well, guess what? I got one of ... They had to hold me down, and Baxter came over and told him, "You have to pay him, because he did what you bet he could do."

Anthony: So, after World War II, did you stay in the service? You got discharged.

Manuel: I got discharged.

Anthony: You got discharged in 19-

Manuel: '46.

Anthony: January 16th, 1946.

Manuel: January 5th, wasn't it?

Anthony: I'm not sure, okay, but in January, 1946.

Manuel: Yes, and that's when I was trying to, since I had learned to drive a tractor trailer out there, I got quite a few jobs with a raggedy company, the guy at Blossom nurseries and Lucci's trucking, but he drove all the trucks until they fell apart, and a lot of times you got a ticket for it. They would pull you to the side, that little grade in the Bronx part of New York, and they would tell you to put the hand brake on and get out. So, you'd put the hand brake on, and if she rolled back more than six inches, you got a ticket.

Manuel: They would ask you, "How do you light your flares?" "I know how to light them." He said, "No, you have to have stick matches," because stick matches, you can do it. It was hard to get them not to be dry. It was easy with the pocket matches. You could sweat and stuff, but you couldn't light with that, and you'd get a ticket if you didn't have it. I remember one day I was driving one of the cars off the Whitestone Bridge, and my brakes started failing, coming down to the booth.

Manuel: I was just lucky that one booth was open, and I sailed through that booth and got the car over to the side and kept braking it down to the lowest gear, and rubbing the tires on the curb, and it stopped. Here comes a policeman in his car. He said, "Do you know you didn't pay a toll back there?" I said, "Pay the toll? You're lucky nobody was in that toll booth."

Anthony: Wow, so in between, after your discharge, you went to work as a driver.

Manuel: Yeah, right.

CHAPTER 7
KOREAN WAR

USS Brinkley Bass (DD 887) was deployed to the Korean war zone in 1950. On May 20, 1951 while engaged at Wonsan Harbor enemy shells hit the destroyer. Manuel J. Knox was a hospital corpsman. Knox was the first to see enemy fire an alerted the crew.

Anthony: And then, let's see, rolling along, you enlisted again.

Manuel: Yes.

Anthony: Re-enlisted in the U.S. Navy in, I think it says September 6th, 1950.

Manuel: That's right, and the 26th I was on the U.S. Brinkley Bass.

Anthony: Also known as the DD-887.

Manuel: That's right, U.S. Brinkley Bass, DD-887, and next thing you know, we were in Wonsan Harbor, in North Korea.

Anthony: So that's when you were engaged in the Korean War.

Manuel: Yes, and when I got there, they wanted to know what I wanted to specialize in, so the chief there checked my records and he said, "Well, you could be a good medic."

I said, "Well, I sure will," so I was assigned with two other guys as medics under this Chief Green.

Anthony: Right, so that's typically called the hospital corpsmen.

Manuel: The hospital corpsmen, yeah.

Anthony: Okay, very good, so yeah, there's a big story about the USS Brinkley Bass, right?

Manuel: Yes, we were the first U.S. warship hit in Korea, and we were up in Wonsan Harbor. The commodore, the rank which is now, the rank that, they did away with it. They don't have that rank anymore, but he was commander of destroyer division 52. We had four destroyers, Bass, Duncan, there was four, two more. But anyway, we would make a figure eight in the harbor, and the commodore decided we had too much 40-millimeter ammo aboard, because we wasn't firing at no planes. We was only firing at, we had coordinates that the Marines would send back to our ship.

Manuel: So, me and the corpsmen, with all my first aid boxes and everything were clear, and I checked them every day because some of the guys would try to open them up, because some of the boxes had morphine in them, morphine syrettes and stuff that they would like to have, for what reason I don't know, but anyway, I told this one, "Look out. Go get yourself some coffee." I took his big glasses and was scanning the area, and I recall that bridge port lookout, they're firing at us.

Manuel: The chief down on the front part is saying, same ship, he said, "Knox, get your ass off that bridge, because every time you go on the bridge, we go to general quarters." I said, "Chief, look out there and tell me, do you see the fish jump that high?" About that time, another round hit and they was trying to get to the 105s so they could get us, but we were pretty safe, because we were pointed towards them. So, you've got a long ship like this, but when you turn sideways, you've got ...

Manuel: Off the deck, sound in general quarters, that means the guys working the engine room got to get down there fast and get it going, and the guys in the first division have got to get that big ass anchor up, so they're pulling the anchor up, and the anchor got hooked to something, and they can't move. At the same time, they can't move, the engine room finally got the engines going, and they started pulling, and they pulled us around and we were broadside, and they hit us at midship.

Manuel: We lost one, and about 19 injured, and most all of them was in the positions where they weren't supposed to be. When you receive fire from shore batteries, all the guys that were not on the 105 guns had to be inside of the border alleyways and stuff on the ship, but they were not supposed to be outside. That's when they hit us on midship, the shrapnel is what wounded so many guys.

Anthony: Oh yeah, right.

Manuel: We called for help, and we called for one wounded. He was Dr. Van Sickel doctor of my corpsmen. I said, "Nothing wrong with me, Doc." You can't use a stretcher on them little small ships, but they taught us to use stretchers, and I carried him like the fireman's carry across my shoulders, and dragged him over, and then the other guys helped me get him up to the next deck. When we got him up there, he was in bad shape. We have a highline, and the highline cruiser, no but it was a cruiser, anyway. She turned in, and she throws this line to us, and we throw our line back, and they get it hooked up so baskets going across. The guys are running up and down the deck. When we wanted to bring him towards them, we run one way of the deck, and then when they want to bring the basket back, they run the same way.

Manuel: Okay, and every time the ships sort of dipped away from each other, but they weren’t supposed to be going in the same rhythm, that guy in the basket went right down in the water and came back up, and it was rough, but we got him on the other ship, but he died on the cruiser.

Anthony: So, there was one killed and several injured.

Manuel: Yeah, about 18, 19 wounded, and all of that wounded was, they were out there trying to take pictures of the near misses. When they finally found me, I was at the bottom of the sick bay, where all the medicine and stuff was, covered up. They couldn't go through two bulkheads to get to me.

Anthony: Wow, that's quite a story.

Manuel: We pulled to the side, and we were there for a short while longer, but we noticed that all the places where the shells hit, they didn't let us paint them gray. They made them, we call that, we had a substance called red lead.

Anthony: So, it's a primer or something?

Manuel: Yes.

Anthony: Right, okay.

Manuel: And you keep that out so they could see, when we pull into San Diego, they're going to see the warship come home.

Anthony: So, you were the first ship to take on enemy fire in-

Manuel: No, we weren't the first ship to take on. We were the first ship hit.

Anthony: The first ship hit.

Manuel: Yeah.

Anthony: Okay.

Manuel: Hit by it.

Anthony: Wow, quite an experience.

Manuel: Yeah.

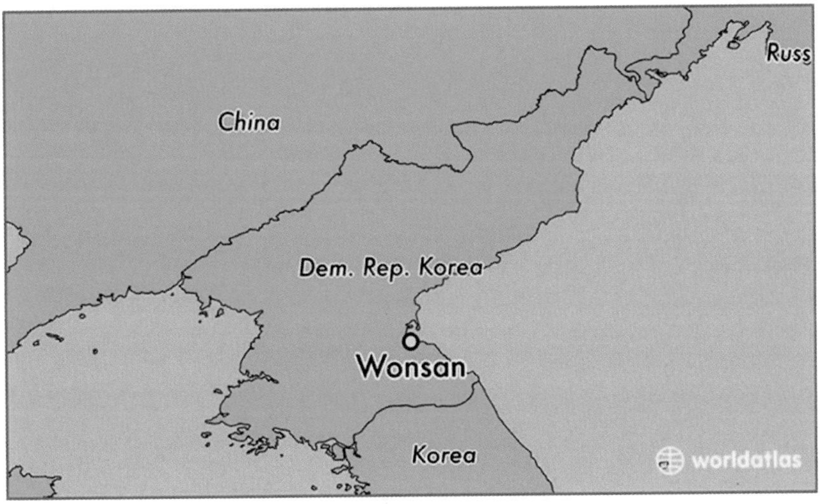

Wonsan Harbor, North Korea

Anthony: So, let's see, so then the Korean War, after ... So, you were on the Brinkley until 19 ..., so the Brinkley, the Bass came back home shortly after that, right?

Manuel: Right.

Anthony: Back to San Diego.

Manuel: Yeah.

Anthony: Right, and then your next assignment was-

Manuel: St. Albans

Anthony: Yeah, where was that?

CHAPTER 8
MEDICAL TRAINING AND OTHER MEDICAL ASSIGNMENTS

St Allbans Naval Hospital, Jamaica, NY, Knox attended X-ray program at the hospital training school

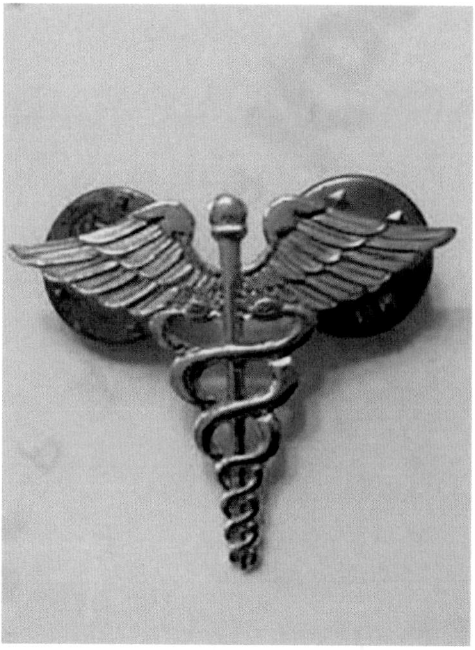

Caduceus (symbol of medicine)

Manuel: St. Albans, Long Island, New York. It's a golf course now. Back then it was a naval training station.

Anthony: Yeah, so it's a ... I think you said it was a U.S. naval hospital.

Manuel: It was a hospital, yeah. It was a hospital.

Anthony: And you-

Manuel: I went to x-ray school.

Anthony: X-ray school, yeah, okay, very good. Wow, so that must have been quite an experience.

Manuel: Yes, it was.

Anthony: All right, so then you followed, after that you went to one of your favorite assignments.

Manuel: San Juan, Puerto Rico.

Anthony: San Juan, Puerto Rico, so what was that like? It looks like you said the naval dispensary.

Manuel: Right, that was right next to the air station that you would come into Puerto Rico, and we had regular assignments. I did x-rays there, and one time the fellow in charge of, what's it called? Environmental protection, I had to go up to certain bars in town and take specimens of milk and water, and if the e. coli was high, I closed them down.

Anthony: Oh, okay.

Manuel: And so when I went out at night for liberty, they would think I was checking them, and they would give me just free drinks, oh, man.

Anthony: So this was part of the Navy's effort to protect the soldiers when they were out.

Manuel: Because the Navy protected that port, where stop 17 was. Stop seven and a half, rather, and now you had the police out there, called the air base, Roosevelt Field. All the guys in Puerto Rico in service, we did all the physicals for FBI agents in Puerto Rico. They would send the guys down there, and they would go through training down there, and we had to make sure they had shots. Then when I left, how long did I stay in Puerto Rico?

Anthony: I think you ... What was it? I know you said you wanted, you tried very hard to get an extension.

Manuel: Oh, I did. I did, I enjoyed the station so much, the first extension I put in for they allowed me. That's why in my record there it looks like I was at the same place twice.

Anthony: Right, yeah.

Manuel: And I enjoyed that.

Anthony: But no third time, no third extension.

Manuel: No, they said, "You can't stay no longer."

Anthony: So, then you went to ... Tell us about your next assignment. I think it was military sea transport service.

Brooklyn Army Terminal located in Brooklyn, NY-home of Military Sea Transportation Service (MSTS). Knox a X-ray technician assigned to MSTS and provided medical services to sailors and their dependents across Europe with frequent ocean travel.

Manuel: MSTS.

Anthony: And that was in Brooklyn.

Manuel: Yes, Brooklyn Army Terminal.

Anthony: Right, so you were an x-ray technician there?

Manuel: Yes, well remember at that Brooklyn Army Terminal, you were assigned to a ship. These ships only had a complement of 30 military personnel. The rest of the personnel are civil service workers, Merchant Marines.

Anthony: Oh, okay, Merchant Marines.

Manuel: Yeah, they served you good dinners and good food and everything.

Anthony: So these were supply ships-

Manuel: Yeah.

Anthony: That were going out.

Manuel: Take the whole family, if a sergeant and his family went, they had state rooms. The rest of the troops would go down below.

Anthony: Okay, so you would go out on these, across the Atlantic trips, then.

Manuel: Yes, seven days between New York and Southampton, England. We would leave New York on Monday, and the Queen Mary probably left two days later. The third day, I would see the Queen Mary would pass us. It took them like three, three and a half days to go across, and it took us seven days. I got a commendation from, one of the little boys caught the croup, and I volunteered to stay out of my state room, to stay in the hospital section with that little boy.

Manuel: They had a machine that you could keep it running good, and keep the air good for that patient. It had to be furnished with ice like every two or three hours, so

I made my bunk in the hospital section there. Seven days later, when we got to Southampton and his family was getting off, he didn't want to leave me. The father and mother sent a nice letter into the cardinal, and they were from Cornwall, New York, about how much they relied on me, because they had about five or six kids, yeah.

Anthony: Oh, so you took care of the sick kid.

Manuel: Yeah.

Anthony: Okay, so very good. That's quite a story of going back and forth across the Atlantic, so these ships were supplying the Naval-

Manuel: Personnel.

Anthony: Personnel across in Europe.

Manuel: Yeah.

Anthony: Wow, so quite a story.

Manuel: Once we got to Southampton, England, the families going there got off. Then we went across the channel to Bremerhaven, Germany, and let some off. We'd go around the horn to the Straits of Gibraltar and go to, the first stop was Leghorn, Italy, Naples, Italy, Izmir, Turkey, Piraeus, Greece, and then do the whole thing all the way back to New York.

Anthony: Wow, quite a-

Manuel: That was quite a trip.

Anthony: So that was like 14 days at sea, huh?

Manuel: Oh, yeah. It was more than that, because when we got into ... There was one incident where we got into Piraeus, Greece, and we were getting on our clothes, going to go in town, and get this cab. The cabbie's got one guy holding the wheel, holding the bamboo strips, and six, eight guys get on there. It makes no difference, they could really roll. If a cabbie hit something, you get off, you have to run. Say, "Why do you have to run?" "If they catch whoever hired the taxi, he has to pay the fine." The guys were running, and I'm standing there. The guys said, "Come on, man." I was at the front of the group, and that's when I found out that you have to pay for the damage that that guy caused.

Anthony: Because you hired the taxi.

Manuel: Yes, because we hired it. Piraeus, Greece, was the prettiest harbor of all the harbors. I'll tell you, it was so gorgeous. You sailed into the harbor, the houses on the hills, the flowers and everything was great. What is that?

Anthony: That's this thing.

Manuel: Oh, that's that thing. I thought it was my phone.

Anthony: No.

Manuel: Okay, and ...

Anthony: So, that was quite an assignment.

Manuel: Yeah.

NRD PHILADELPHIA

Anthony: So, then you went from MSTS to Philadelphia.

Manuel: Yeah.

Anthony: In May, 1961.

Manuel: What's the name of the Philadelphia?

Anthony: Oh, so but after, so let's break here for a second. So after MTST, you discharged from the Navy, after you left MTST ... What is it? MSTS.

Manuel: MSTS.

Anthony: You discharged from the Navy, or did you go to Philadelphia after MSTS?

Manuel: MSTS, then I went to ... No.

Anthony: Okay, so after you left MSTS in Brooklyn, you went to Philadelphia, home of brotherly love.

Manuel: Yes.

Anthony: The city of brotherly love, and what was your ... And that was in May, 1961.

Manuel: Right, and then I was in charge of the medical section there. It was the first time in my military career that I had men who outranked me, but I was the lead medical officer in charge. This was due to the fact that the school that you go through for the Navy had more extensive and longer training.

Anthony: Okay, very good.

Manuel: So, when I got to the recruiting, because actually you're on recruiting duty. For instance, I had to have knowledge of all the different stations in the medical section, because you would know if a guy was doing his job good. Lots of times when I went out at night at a club in Philly and the guys would say, "There's that guy that put me in the service." I didn't do it. I didn't put you in the service. You passed with flying colors to get in there. Funniest thing, most of the black enlistees would come in and want to get exempted because of flat feet, and it was no good. All the runners that ever did anything, good running, still had flat feet, because they didn't have shoes, so they ran with them, so their flat feet could not exempt them from service.

Anthony: They passed the medical exam.

Manuel: Yes.

Anthony: So, wow, that should have been quite a deal.

Manuel: Yeah.

Anthony: So let's see, so you were home in Philadelphia.

Manuel: Yes.

Anthony: And then you went to ... And let's see, when? In May 1964, or excuse me, December 1964.

Manuel: Yeah.

Anthony: You went to the Bureau of Medicine and Surgery Advanced Hospital Corps School.

Manuel: In Portsmouth, Virginia.

Anthony: Port?

Manuel: Portsmouth.

Anthony: Virginia.

Manuel: Yes.

Anthony: Okay, then that's your famous B school.

Manuel: Oh, yeah. When you graduate from this school, you are excelling in medical service, and they gave you a certificate that said that you are qualified to do medical duties independent of a medical officer. However, a medical officer was always within your grip or within your communicated branch to give you, to assess what you decided to do for whatever patient you had.

Anthony: Wow.

Manuel: I could start broad spectrum antibiotics. I could do minor surgery, except for the face, and dispense medication to the fellows. That was pretty proud.

Anthony: Wow, that's great. That's like a physician's assistant today.

Manuel: Yes.

Anthony: Wow.

Manuel: And that school entailed getting up, going to class at 7:30, you went to eat breakfast. Eight o'clock you was in class until 4:30 every day for six solid months, including Saturday and Sunday.

Anthony: Wow, that's pretty extensive.

Manuel: Yes.

Anthony: So that's your most proudest-

Manuel: Award.

Anthony: Award.

Manuel: Yes.

Anthony: Wow, quite an honor.

Manuel: Yeah.

Anthony: Quite an honor.

Manuel: Thank you.

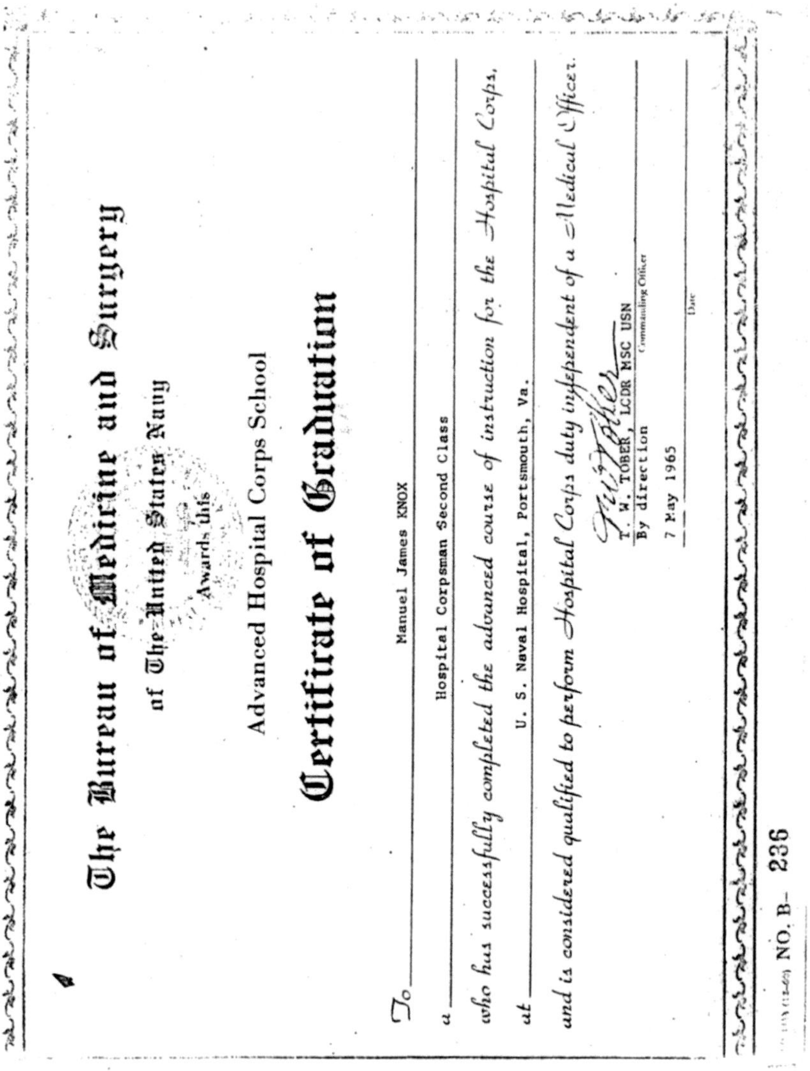

The Bureau of Medicine and Surgery
of The United States Navy
Awards this
Advanced Hospital Corps School
Certificate of Graduation

To Manuel James KNOX

a Hospital Corpsman Second Class

who has successfully completed the advanced course of instruction for the Hospital Corps,

at U. S. Naval Hospital, Portsmouth, Va.

and is considered qualified to perform Hospital Corps duty independent of a Medical Officer.

T. W. TOBER, LCDR MSC USN
By direction
Commanding Officer

7 May 1965
Date

NO. B- 236

Manuel Knox receives Certification of Graduation for Hospital Corpsman Second Class, at The Bureau of Medicine and Surgery, Portsmouth, VA, May 1, 1965

Anthony: Quite an honor. So then, let's see, what happened after that? You went to, let's see, you went to San Francisco. So then you, what happened after that? You tell me.

Manuel: Then, I was received for duty instruction at U.S. Naval ... Oh, we did talk about the naval hospital.

Anthony: Right.

Manuel: And from there, the guys in my class ... Okay, so yeah, when I left the hospital, I went to the field medical service with the Marines, so I was assigned to the first battalion, third Marine division, and went through training with the Marines, because the medics had to be able to know how to bring an injured person in, and how to be safe out there, so I was out with them from '64 to ... As soon as I did finish the classes there, we were assigned with the third Marine division in Vietnam.

CHAPTER 9
VIETNAM WAR

3rd Marine Division, Vietnam. Knox was assigned to 3rd Division, Company B as a Hospital Corpsman (Medic) on the front lines of the Vietnam War 1965-66

Anthony: Oh, okay, so let me make sure we've got this right. So, after you did B school, from B school, you went to field training to prepare ...

Manuel: To go with the Marines.

Anthony: To go with the Marines, and then after that, that was in San Diego, then after that assignment, you were with the third Marine division, and you were assigned to Vietnam.

Manuel: Yes.

Anthony: Wow, okay, so tell me about Vietnam. So, you, I heard you had some challenges there with being right there in the fire.

Manuel: Oh, yes. One thing that I do remember, a petty officer in charge, and the doctors stayed in one tent. We built our own tents, and one night we were playing cards and a couple of rounds went off. Everybody hit the dirt. I crawled to my foxhole, as the doctors and the other medics did, too. When everything got quiet, two Marines, there was no enemy there, but two Marines was fighting over a 3.2 can of beer, that you know they got, when the sergeants finally found out who it was, they got a lot of extra duty done to them.

Anthony: Right, so you were leading a medic team, right?

Manuel: Yes.

Anthony: You were the leader of a medic team, so tell us about what that ... I think you said you got there, and shortly after you got there that you ...

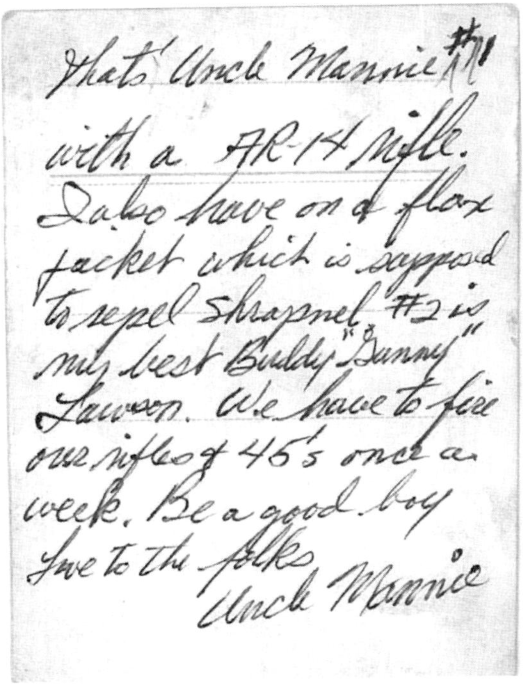

That's Uncle Mannie #1
with a AR-14 rifle.
I also have on a flax
jacket which is supposed
to repel shrapnel, #2 is
my best Buddy "Sunny"
Lawson. We have to fire
our rifles & 45's once a
week. Be a good boy
Love to the folks
Uncle Mannie

Hospital Corpsman Knox on duty in Vietnam with a personal message to his nephew

Manuel: Yeah, well, we wasn't there too much, and we lost three Marines, corpsmen, the medics.

Anthony: Yeah, corpsmen medics.

Manuel: And Lampman, who was the only medic I had left, and he was a member, his family, he was a millionaire too, and he was a corpsman. I told Lampman that I would alternate with him until a replacement got in, which took 30 days. That's where I quit smoking, because at 4:30 in the afternoon, the Marines are getting ready to go out. You go out from 4:30 in the afternoon, all night until 7:30 the next morning. However, you sat in bivouac. It took an hour to go sit in, to be in a place that you can see the enemy, and the enemy can't see you.

Manuel: We sat in places that we passed three times that was there. I said, "Well, how come you do it so many?" He said, "The enemies not supposed to know where you are, and so you have to do that." So, we had one corpsman who wanted to be a Marine so bad. He was there with the Marines, and I know that guys go to sleep on watch, and he noticed that everybody was asleep except him, because he's supposed to go walk, go around and see if the guys need anything.

Manuel: He saw that the sergeant in charge of the unit was asleep, so he took his grenade, pulled the pin, threw it a short distance away from him, and prostrated himself over the sergeant. When it went off, everybody was confusion and everything else. One of the guys said the sergeant was thinking about giving him an award, and the guy still had the pin from the grenade on his hand, so the next day he was transferred to Japan, because they don't need nobody like that aboard, right?

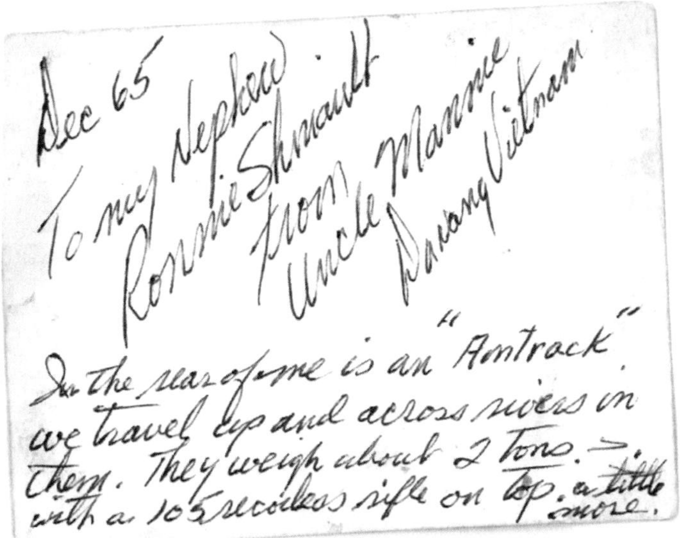
Dec 65
To my Nephew
Ronnie Shmault
from
Uncle Mannie
Danang Vietnam

In the rear of me is an "Amtrack".
we travel up and across rivers in
them. They weigh about 2 Tons. –>
with a 105 recoilless rifle on top. a little more.

Knox in Da Nang, Vietnam, keeps in touch with his nephew

Philly Marine Good Samaritan *to Vietnam Boy*

Anthony: Right, so I was reading an article in the Philadelphia Inquirer about, it says Philly Marine Samaritan to Vietnam boy. Good Samaritan Marine Manuel Knox of Philadelphia shown in Vietnam where he has become favored with natives because of his work on aiding underprivileged children. Tell us about that. You're in a war zone-

Manuel: Yes, we are, and whenever Marines settled an area, and no VC were in the area, then we would have a medical team go out to the little villages there and service the people that got hurt from the VC and maybe from some of our rounds. However, we saw this little boy named Luke, and Luke's foot was turned I would say 20 to 40 degrees in the wrong direction. Dr. Shady decided that we'd bring him in, manipulate his leg a small amount of degrees every day that he came to the base camp. I know his foot never got around to the normal thing, but when we left that area, Luke's foot was about 70%-

Anthony: Wow.

Manuel: Facing the right direction. We would take the cast off and turn it, boy, and he would holler, but he was a good little boy. We'd put the cast on, and we'd have to keep it still until it started to harden. When we felt it was hard enough, then we would let him get on his little crutches and go back into town.

Anthony: Wow.

Manuel: And the kids enjoyed us giving them ... We would have one of the big syringes, we'd put cough syrup in it and give them a little squirt of cough syrup. It was just like giving them a piece of candy.

Anthony: Candy, right.

Manuel: Most of their injuries was cured with Ivory soap and water.

Anthony: Wow.

Manuel: But they would have, I don't know why they ever did that, but when they got hurt out in the fields, and this went for the grown people, they would take cow dung and put it on the area, and it would harden, but yet they had these ugly marks on their legs and their arms from it. It would heal, but that stuff was still there in their skin. Whenever we went into a village and we'd be serving them, Dr. Shady and two other medics, we would serve the people.

Manuel: They would notice that all of a sudden, the people were gone. They would leave our area whenever that happened. The VC was in the area. We relieved the division corps 27, and one of the guys had his own shotgun, and I purchased it from him. He was going back to the States, and we was relieving his company. He said, "I'll sell it to you." I said, "Okay, I want it," because I had a .45. The medics aren't supposed to be armed, according to the Geneva Convention, but we were armed. I knew this .45 with this shotgun, if I fired at you, I'm going to hit you with it. A .45, I don't see where I could hit the side of a barn with it, because it gave you such a kick when you shoot it.

Anthony: Wow, that was a tremendous thing that you guys were doing for the locals, in providing them medical care.

Manuel: Yeah, we built our tent for them, but in an area, you could see that local Seabees unit, Seabees built us a real good-looking hospital. Did you see that?

Anthony: Right, so that was-

Manuel: That was the old one, that we put up, but this is what the Seabees put up for us. We really had a wonderful hospital.

Anthony: Wonderful, what a humanitarian thing to do.

Manuel: Yes.

GOOD SAMARITAN. . . Marine Manuel Knox, of Philadelphia shown in Vietnam, where he has become favorite with natives because of his work on aiding under-privileged children.

Philly Marine Samaritan To Vietnam Boy

Thanks to the individual efforts of Philadelphia's Manuel Knox, marines in Vietnam are doing very well with a big portion of the populace argund the town of Da Nang.

The other day a 12-year old Vietnamese boy hobbled to the door of the Marine medical aid station and fell on his face in the mud-but none of the-watching marines and medical corpsmen moved to help him.

Then the boy, nicknamed "Luke", hauled himself to his feet with the aid of his crutches and the small smile expanded into a full grin as the marines and corpsmen offered their congratulations.

Luke is a special friend of the men of the 1st Bn., 3d Marine Regt. Navy hospital corpsman 1C Manuel Knox of Philadelphia, was the first to spot him.

Luke used to sit in the market place of a nearby village, his club foot folded under him, his crude crutches at his side, watching as the other children played.

Now a jeep arrives at the market place every morning and Luke is taken to the battalion aid station.

The battalion medical officer, Navy Lt. Edward J. Shahady of Fairmont, W. Va., has fitted a special brace to Luke's deformed foot and the foot is slowly being forced into a normal position.

Philadelphia Inquiry newspaper article on Knox' humanitarian contributions

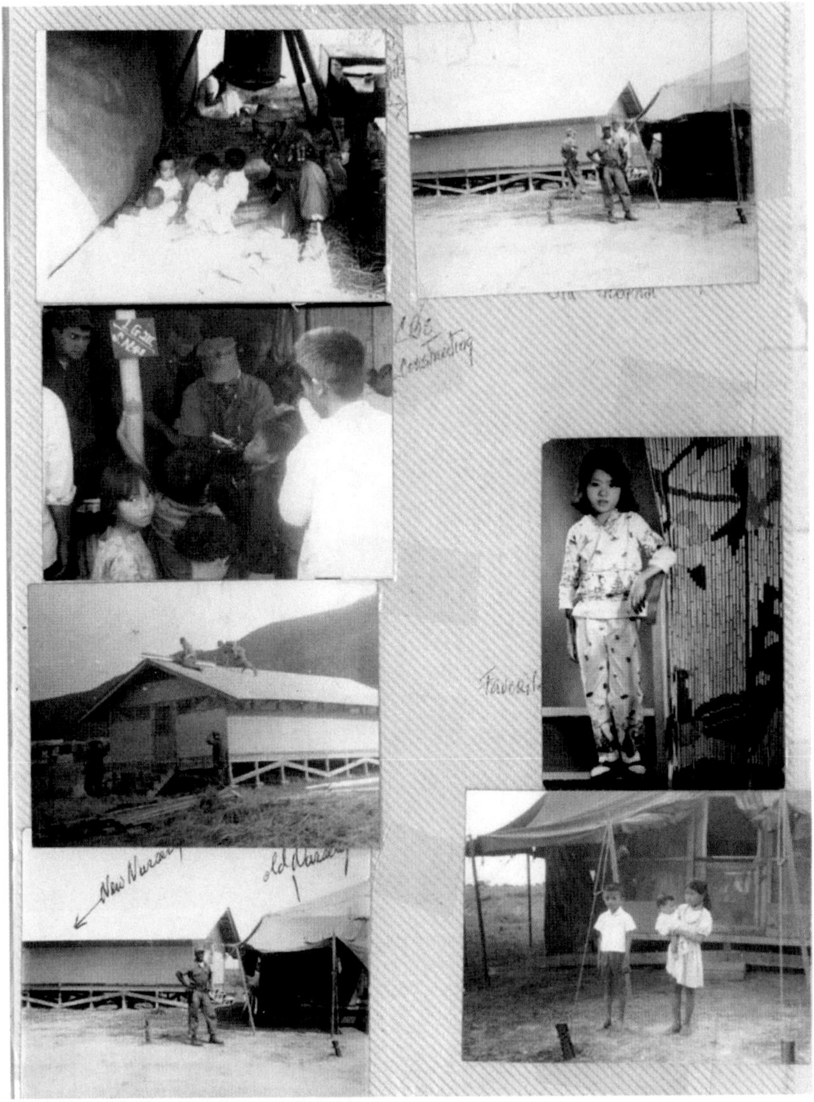

Knox providing medical care and humanitarian care to children of Vietnam

Petty Officer First Class Manuel Knox and wife Madge attending Awards Ceremony on his last day of Military Service, January 5, 1968

CHAPTER 10
MILITARY SERVICES AWARD

Meritorious Service Award

World War II Victory Medal

Korea Service Medal

Vietnam Service Medal

Anthony: So, let's see, now so you've gone through all of this, and then along the way you had awards, ribbons, citations, commendations. I was reading somewhere that you had 27.

Manuel: Yeah.

Anthony: So, you had some from, let's see, the good conduct medals from World War II.

Manuel: Yeah.

Anthony: The victory medal, the American champion medal, the Asiatic Pacific campaign medal. Then, you had the national defense service medal.

Manuel: Yeah.

Anthony: Let's see, then you had the Korean service medal, United Nations service medal, the Korean defense service medal, the Presidential unit citation. Oh, excuse me, you also had the Vietnam service medal.

Manuel: Yes.

Anthony: And then you had the combat action, and you had several awards. This is wonderful. Thanks again for your wonderful service. So, that will be included. We'll include that, and so the other thing is, then you spent 23 years' total time in the military, spanned over three wars.

Manuel: Mm-hmm (affirmative).

Anthony: Wow, and you left the military in 1968.

MILITARY SERVICES AWARD

Decorations, Medals, Badges, Commendations, Citations and Campaign Ribbons

Branch	US Navy	
Service Member	Manuel (Manny) James Knox	

Award	Description	Details	Other
Medal	Meritorious Service Medal		
Medal	Good Conduct Medal	Navy	With 4 bronze stars
Medal	World War II Victory Medal		
Medal	American Campaign Medal		
Medal	Astatic Pacific Campaign Medal		
Medal	National Defense Service Medal		With 1 bronze stars
Medal	Korean Service Medal		With 4 bronze stars
Medal	United Nations Service Medal		
Medal	Expeditionary Medal	Navy	
Medal	Korean Defense Service Medal		
Medal	Vietnam Service Medal		
Ribbon	Presidential Unit Citation Ribbon		
Ribbon	Meritorious Unit Commendation Ribbon		
Ribbon	Combat Action Ribbon		

Award	Description	Details	Other
Pin	Honorable Service Lapel Pin		Ruptured Duck
Button	Honorable Discharge Button		
Medal	Republic of Korea War Service Medal		
Ribbon	SEA Service Deployment Ribbon		
Ribbon	Navy/MARCOR Overseas Service Ribbon		
Medal	USN/USCG Arctic Service Medal		
Citation	Presidential Unit Citation	Republic of Korea	
Citation	Presidential Unit Citation	Vietnam	
Citation	Republic of Vietnam Meritorious Unit Citation	Vietnam	Gallantry Cross Medal with Color Palm

Chapter 11
Retired from Military

Anthony: Okay, so that's wonderful. Then, when you left the military, you took on some jobs as an x-ray technician. You worked at Lourdes Hospital. You worked at-

Manuel: Rancocas.

Anthony: Rancocas.

Manuel: And then the VA hospital first, then got transferred over to the Rancocas Hospital. From Rancocas Hospital, I found out that I still was working at the VA hospital, and at the VA, they want me to pay the two taxes, Pennsylvania and New Jersey, so I had to come on over to New Jersey, period. I was working for a short while at Rancocas, and the chief at Rancocas Hospital, Rocky and I, went to classes at Hahnerman

University Hospital (Philadelphia PA), for an associate degree in radiological health.

Institute For Radiologic Technologists

This is to certify that

MANUEL JAMES KNOX R.T.

has attended the Institute
for Radiologic Technologists conducted by
The American Society of Radiologic Technologists
In cooperation with
The American College of Radiology
The American Hospital Association
The American Registry of Radiologic Technologists

Executive Secretary
The American Society of Radiologic Technologists

Director
The American Hospital Association

Executive Director
The American College of Radiology

Executive Director
The American Registry of Radiologic Technologists

1971

DAYTON, OHIO

Manuel: We put in for employment at Rancocas Hospital, and he got the job because he accepted the smaller salary. After accepting the smaller salary, I stayed at the VA in Philly, and he called me and said, "I need an assistant chief." So, I said, "Are you going to give me that salary I requested with the other one?" He said, "Yeah." I said, "Well then, I'll be over." I came over and became a, joined the State of New Jersey X-ray Society Unit.

State of New York X-Ray Technician License

State of New York Department of Health

EACH LICENSEE MUST CONSPICUOUSLY DISPLAY THIS CERTIFICATE IN HIS PRINCIPAL PLACE OF EMPLOYMENT AT ALL TIMES TOGETHER WITH HIS LICENSE IT CONSTITUTES HIS AUTHORITY TO PRACTICE DURING THE CURRENT PERIOD. IN THE EVENT OF A CHANGE OF ADDRESS RETURN THIS CERTIFICATE FOR CORRECTION.

THIS IS TO CERTIFY THAT

LICENSE NO. 121168651

MANUEL J KNOX, L.X.T.
32 PEMBROOK LANE
WILLINGBORO, NJ 08046

HAVING MET THE STATUTORY REQUIREMENTS OF THE STATE OF NEW YORK IS ENTITLED TO THIS CERTIFICATE OF REGISTRATION AS AN

X-RAY TECHNICIAN

THIS CERTIFICATE IS DATED JANUARY 1, 1970 AND EXPIRES DECEMBER 31, 1971

Howard S. Goldman, L.X.T.
Secretary, X-ray Technician Board of Examiners

Hollis S. Ingraham, M.D.
Commissioner of Health

XT-8 No. A 06932

State of New York Department of Health

EACH LICENSEE MUST CONSPICUOUSLY DISPLAY THIS CERTIFICATE IN HIS PRINCIPAL PLACE OF EMPLOYMENT AT ALL TIMES. TOGETHER WITH HIS LICENSE IT CONSTITUTES HIS AUTHORITY TO PRACTICE DURING THE CURRENT PERIOD. IN THE EVENT OF A CHANGE OF ADDRESS RETURN THIS CERTIFICATE FOR CORRECTION.

THIS IS TO CERTIFY THAT

LICENSE NO. 121128651

MANUEL J KNOX
32 PEMBROOK LANE
WILLINGBORO, NEW JERSEY 08046

HAVING MET THE STATUTORY REQUIREMENTS OF THE STATE OF NEW YORK IS ENTITLED TO THIS CERTIFICATE OF REGISTRATION AS AN

X-RAY TECHNICIAN

THIS CERTIFICATE IS DATED JANUARY 1, 1968 AND EXPIRES DECEMBER 31, 1969

Howard S. Goldman, L.X.T.
Secretary, X-ray Technician Board of Examiners

Hollis S. Ingraham, M.D.
Commissioner of Health

XT-6 Nº 17228

Mr. and Mrs. Manuel Knox attending New Jersey X-Ray Technician Association Annual Conference/Dinner

Anthony: So, you became a chief or a head of that association.

Manuel: Yes, for the state of New Jersey, and we had-

Anthony: That was the X-ray Technician's Association?

X-Ray Technician Association of New Jersey Annual Dinner attended by Association President Manuel J Knox and his beautiful wife Madge H. Knox (on right and 2nd right)

Manuel: Yes, for the state of New Jersey.

Anthony: Great.

Manuel: And we had our regular banquets at the Howard Johnson's in Atlantic City.

Anthony: Oh, okay.

Manuel: Just come over, the first one we came to is Howard Johnson's. Not anymore, but that was quite-

Anthony: That was quite a deal.

Manuel: Yeah.

Anthony: So, let's see, then I understand also since you left the military, you have joined several military organizations, American Legion.

Manuel: The American Legion.

Anthony: The DAV.

Manuel: Chapter 42 in Willingboro, and the VFW. I joined the VFW while I was still in the service, the American Legion while still in the service.

Elmer Knox (Brother of Manuel Knox). Elmer is a Navy Veteran and was a strong advocate for Veterans with the American Legion Post in Yonkers, NY. The brothers were in basic training together at Great Lakes, Illinois during World War II

CHAPTER 12
ADVOCATING FOR VETERANS

Anthony: Okay, and I understand you're a huge advocate for veterans.

Manuel: Yes, indeed, very much so. When I run into a veteran and he hasn't put in for some of his benefits, it disturbs me because they served Uncle Sam, and Uncle Sam does want to serve you, but he can't do anything unless you apply for those benefits, yeah.

Anthony: Right, so I read somewhere that-

Anthony: So, I read somewhere that you helped support the legislative in the state of New Jersey for emergency medical technicians, so that if they had military training, that they could, that would automatically give them a waiver from taking an additional examination.

Manuel: They told me I had to go to school for that. I just dropped the ball and said, "No."

Anthony: So, but that legislation did finally get passed, and so now-

Manuel: Yeah, so they can.

Anthony: They can, they'll get waived. They don't have to do that additional training.

Manuel: Yes.

Anthony: They'll recognize the military training, very good. So, one more question.

Anthony: So, one more question. Is there anything else I haven't asked you about the challenges of serving in three wars, and your military time, that you would like to share, you think is important and you would like to share it?

Manuel: Not at this time

Anthony: Okay, I want to give a salute and shout out to you, Manuel(Manny) James Knox, on behalf of my fellow Americans, for your dedicated service to our nation, and your 22 years of military service including World War II, Korea and Vietnam wars. You are a special human being and a national asset, and we salute you. Thank you for allowing us to uncover your story. I'm sure that your family, friends and fellow veterans will appreciate your priceless story. Again, thank you for sharing. Today, we have captured your memories, so that your story can live forever in history. For your courage, sacrifice and honor, we salute you, Manuel(Manny) James Knox, a veteran of three wars.

DOCUMENT GALLERY

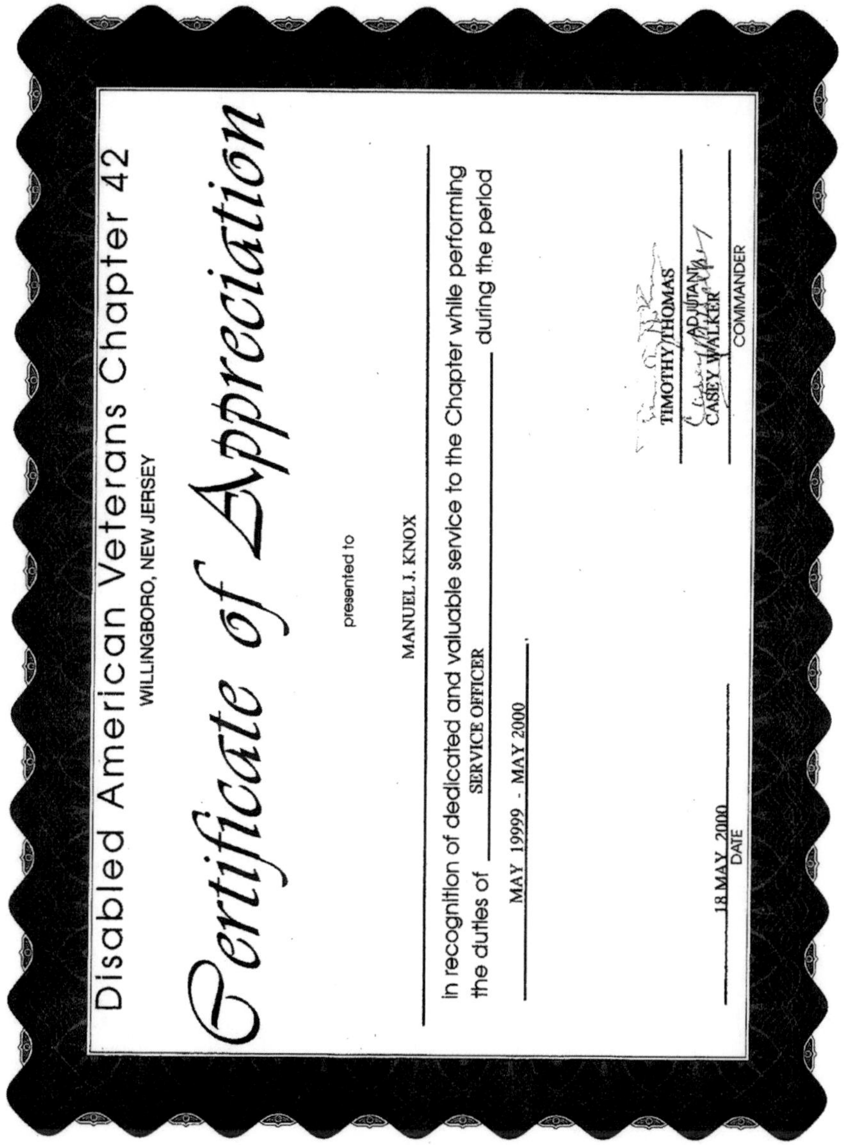

Disabled American Veterans Chapter 42
WILLINGBORO, NEW JERSEY

Certificate of Appreciation

presented to

MANUEL J. KNOX

in recognition of dedicated and valuable service to the Chapter while performing the duties of SERVICE OFFICER during the period

MAY 19999 - MAY 2000.

18 MAY 2000
DATE

TIMOTHY THOMAS
ADJUTANT

CASEY WALKER
COMMANDER

New Jersey
Department of Military and Veterans' Affairs

Certificate of Appreciation

is awarded to

PETTY OFFICER FIRST CLASS MANUEL J. KNOX

In recognition of

For outstanding meritorious service in ground combat during World War II, The Korean War and The Vietnam Conflict in the Asiatic Pacific and Southeast Asiatic Theaters of Operation.

Date July 1999

The Adjutant General

NJDMAVA Form 672-7 1 APR 90

New Jersey General Assembly

STATE HOUSE, TRENTON, N.J.

ASSEMBLY RESOLUTION

By Assemblymen CONAWAY and SINGLETON

WHEREAS, The General Assembly of the State of New Jersey is pleased to join in honoring and saluting Manuel J. Knox, a highly esteemed longtime resident of the Township of Willingboro, Burlington County, in recognition of his seventy years as an outstanding member of the American Legion; and,

WHEREAS, For seven decades, Manuel J. Knox, who has been a valued member of Westampton Memorial American Legion Post No. 509 for many years, has made significant contributions to the American Legion, exercising strong and effective leadership and inspiring his colleagues and the community to promote programs of benefit to veterans and to appreciate good citizenship and patriotic endeavor; and,

WHEREAS, Manuel J. Knox enlisted in the United States Navy on July 15, 1943, and he served his country with honor and valor during World War II before being discharged in 1946, after which he soon joined American Legion Post No. 1072 in Yonkers; and,

WHEREAS, Manuel J. Knox, who re-enlisted in the United States Armed Forces in September of 1950, studied in x-ray and medic schools, and he served during the Korean War and on the ground with the Marine Corps during the Vietnam War before his retirement in 1968; and,

WHEREAS, Manuel J. Knox lent his skill and expertise as Chief of the X-Ray Department at Rancocas Valley Hospital and as Chief of the X-Ray Department and Director of the School of X-Ray Technology at Our Lady of Lourdes Hospital in Camden before his retirement in 1991, and has been a devoted and faithful congregant of Saint Paul Methodist Church; and,

WHEREAS, It is both proper and fitting that this House join in recognizing Manuel J. Knox, whose seventy years of exemplary membership have earned the praise of his comrades within the American Legion, the gratitude of New Jersey's and America's veterans, and the high regard of the citizenry of this State; now, therefore,

Be It Resolved by the General Assembly of the State of New Jersey:

That this House hereby honors Manuel J. Knox, pays tribute to his meritorious record of service, leadership, and commitment as a member of the American Legion for seventy years, and extends to him sincere best wishes; and,

Be It Further Resolved, That a duly authenticated copy of this resolution, signed by the Speaker and attested by the Clerk, be transmitted to Manuel J. Knox.

VINCENT PRIETO
Speaker of the General Assembly

Attest:

DANA M. BURLEY
Clerk of the General Assembly

Correction: American Legion Post 1072 is 1017 in Yonkers, NY

감사 서한
Letter of Appreciation

대 한 민 국

THE REPUBLIC OF KOREA

6·25전쟁 50주년

THE 50th ANNIVERSARY OF THE KOREAN WAR

June 25, 2000

Dear Veteran

On the occasion of the 50th anniversary of the outbreak of the Korean War, I would like to offer you my deepest gratitude for your noble contribution to the efforts to safeguard the Republic of Korea and uphold liberal democracy around the world. At the same time, I remember with endless respect and affection those who sacrificed their lives for that cause.

We Koreans hold dear in our hearts the conviction, courage and spirit of sacrifice shown to us by such selfless friends as you, who enabled us to remain a free democratic nation.

The ideals of democracy, for which you were willing to sacrifice your all 50 years ago, have become universal values in this new century and millennium.

Half a century after the Korean War, we honor you and reaffirm our friendship, which helped to forge the blood alliance between our two countries. And we resolve once again to work with all friendly nations for the good of humankind and peace in the world.

I thank you once again for your noble sacrifice, and pray for your health and happiness.

Sincerely yours,

signed
Kim Dae-jung
President of the Republic of Korea

감사 서한
Letter of Appreciation

대 한 민 국
THE REPUBLIC OF KOREA

존경하는 참전용사 귀하

6·25전쟁이 발발한지 반세기를 맞아 세계의 자유 민주주의와 대한민국을 수호하는데 기여한 귀하에게 진심으로 감사드립니다. 아울러 고귀한 생명을 바치신 영령앞에 무한한 경의와 추모의 뜻을 표합니다.

대한민국이 오늘날의 자유 민주주의 국가를 유지할 수 있도록 귀하께서 보여주셨던 불굴의 신념과 진정한 용기, 그리고 거룩한 희생정신을 우리는 가슴속 깊이 간직하고 있습니다.

특히 귀하께서 50년전에 몸으로 실천했던 자유민주주의 이념은 이제 새로운 세기, 새 천년을 맞아 세계 인류의 보편적 가치가 되었습니다.

이에 6·25전쟁 50주년을 맞이하여 귀하의 명예를 드높임과 동시에 과거 혈맹으로 맺어졌던 귀하와의 우의를 재다짐하고자 합니다. 아울러 인류의 번영과 평화를 위해 세계 우방들과 함께 노력해 나갈 것입니다.

다시 한번 귀하의 숭고한 헌신에 깊이 감사드리며 행운과 건승을 기원합니다.

감사합니다.

2000년 6월 25일

대 한 민 국 대 통 령 김 대 중

Certificate of Special Congressional Recognition

Presented by Congressman Tom MacArthur to

Manual Knox

in recognition of outstanding and invaluable service to our country.

September 12, 2018

DATE

CONGRESSMAN TOM MACARTHUR

MEMBER OF CONGRESS

Post 7677
NJ

Madge Knox relaxing at home.

Manuel and Madge Knox Enjoying Dinner

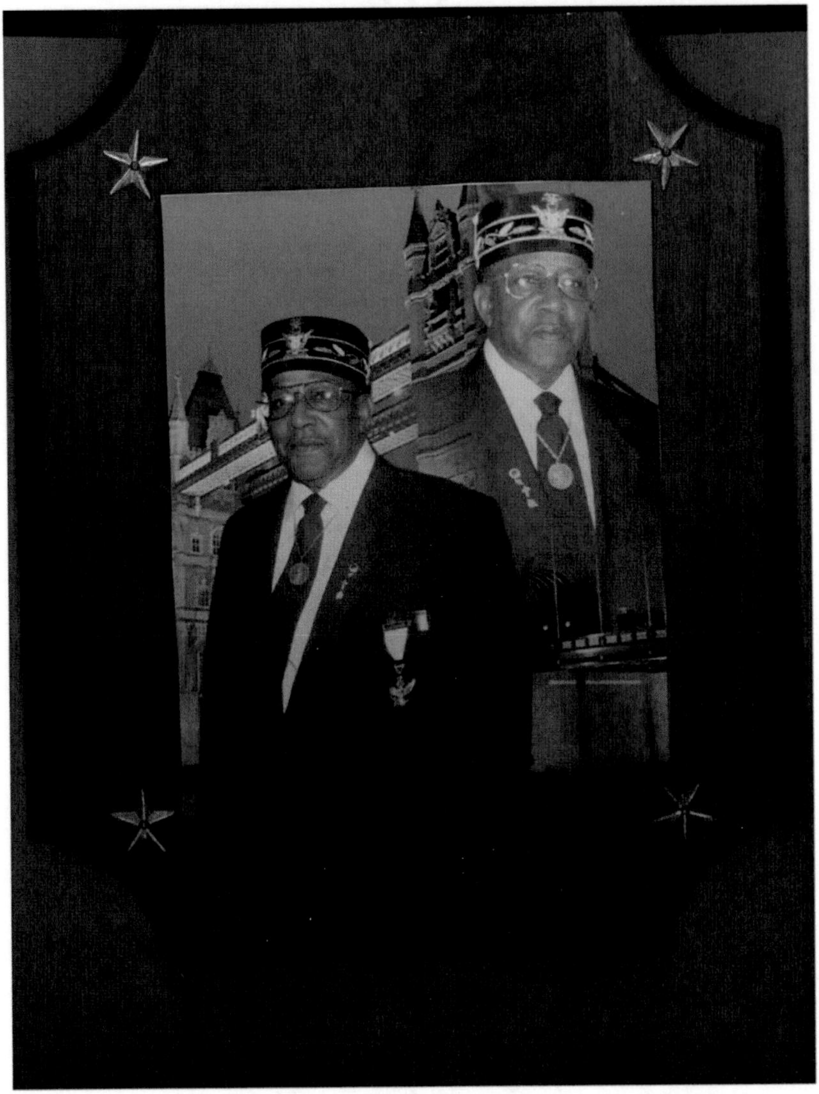

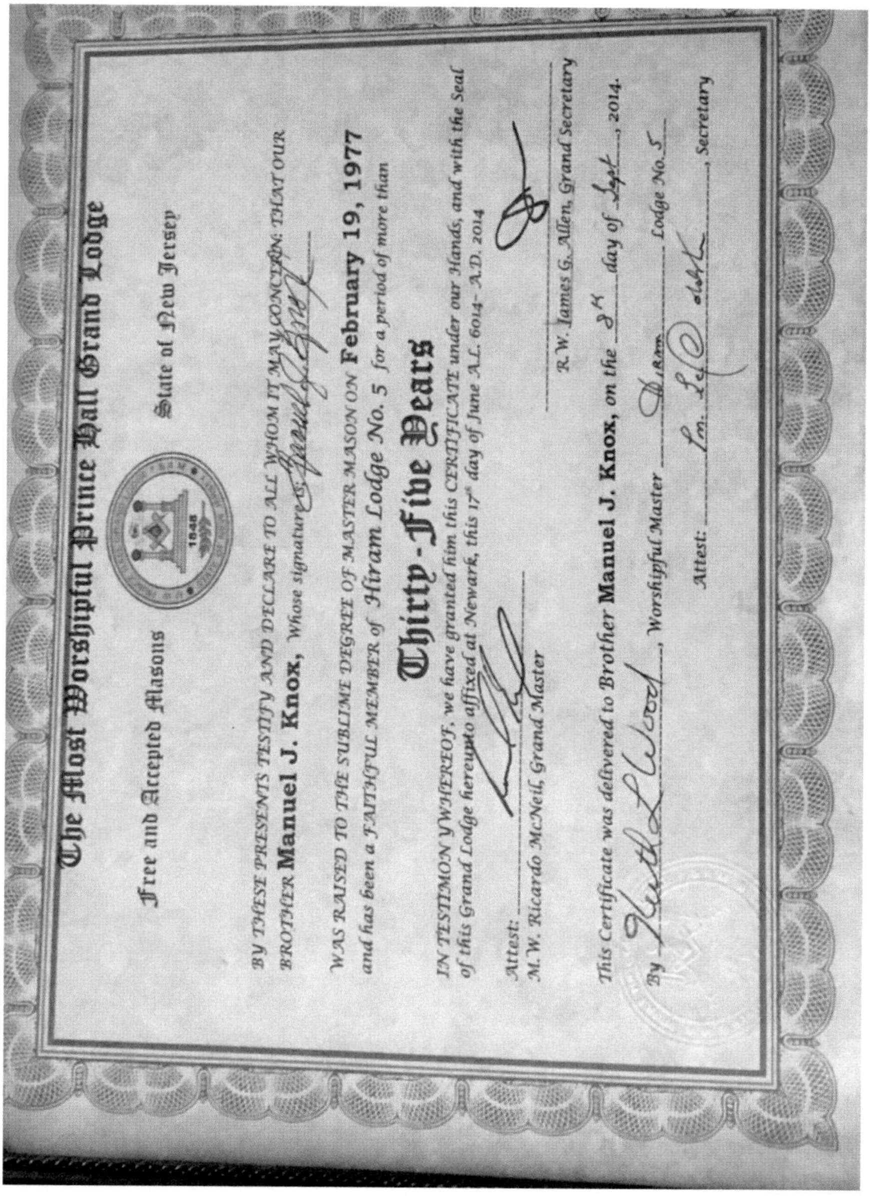

The Most Worshipful Prince Hall Grand Lodge

Free and Accepted Masons — State of New Jersey

BY THESE PRESENTS TESTIFY AND DECLARE TO ALL WHOM IT MAY CONCERN: THAT OUR BROTHER **Manuel J. Knox,** *Whose signature is* ____

WAS RAISED TO THE SUBLIME DEGREE OF MASTER MASON ON **February 19, 1977** *and has been a FAITHFUL MEMBER of* Hiram Lodge No. 5 *for a period of more than*

Thirty-Five Years

IN TESTIMONY WHEREOF, we have granted him this CERTIFICATE under our Hands, and with the Seal of this Grand Lodge hereunto affixed at Newark, this 17th day of June A.L. 6014- A.D. 2014

Attest: ____
M.W. Ricardo McNeil, Grand Master

R.W. James G. Allen, Grand Secretary

This Certificate was delivered to Brother **Manuel J. Knox,** *on the* 8th *day of* Sept, *2014.*

By Keith L Wood, Worshipful Master, Hiram Lodge No. 5

Attest: ____, Secretary

NOTE GALLERY

45797415R00073

Made in the USA
Middletown, DE
21 May 2019